Luogo comune means 'cliché' or 'stereotype' in Italian and is the pseudonym of Jacopo Ghisoni, an illustrator and street artist from Cremona, Italy. As you can tell from his chosen name, his wish, whether illustrating on paper or creating street art on a wall, is to break down stereotypes. On this long voyage across the seven seas, through his images, he brings us secret stories and hidden adventures.

CAMBRIDGESHIRE LIBRARIES	
10010010670713	
Askews & Holts	19-Jan-2023
J623.8	

This English lan...**ing ltd.**

To order a copy or request more information, please visit our website:

www.bsmall.co.uk

Original edition first published in Italian by Sinnos Società Cooperativa.
Original title: *Il grande libro delle navi*
Copyright © 2020 Sinnos
English translation © b small publishing ltd. 2022

1 2 3 4 5 6 7 8 9

ISBN 978-1-913918-39-2

Translator: Catherine Bruzzone
Publisher: Sam Hutchinson
Editorial: Catherine Bruzzone and Sam Hutchinson
Additional design work by Christian Francis and Vicky Barker
Printed in the Czech Republic

Printed on FSC-certified papers produced from sustainable forest/controlled wood sources.

All rights reserved.

No reproduction, copy or transmission of this publication may be made without written permission. No part of this publication may be reproduced, stored in a retrieval system or transmitted in any form or by any means, electronic, mechanical, photocopying, recording or otherwise, without the prior permission of the publisher.

British Library Cataloguing-in-Publication Data. A catalogue record for this book is available from the British Library.

BIG BOOK of *BOATS*

by *Luogo comune*

translated from Italian by Catherine Bruzzone

We all know what a boat is. It is a means of transport that floats on water. But a boat, or ship, is also one of the most important inventions in human history and, like every great invention, it can take very different forms: from the Inuit single kayak or the huge petrol tankers of today, to fishing vessels of every size and even the craft used to explore the world. Are you ready to cast off into the open sea and find out all you can about boats?

1. Gozabune, Japan (1467)

To start with, what is the difference between a boat and a ship? There is no official definition, so it is a question of size. A ship is longer than a boat so, for example, a ship could carry a boat but a boat could not carry a ship.

Icebreaker ship = roughly 100 m or just over 8 buses

Fishing boat = roughly 25 m or 2 lorries

Speedboat = roughly 5 m and up or the size of an average car

Every part of a vessel, on the smallest boat to the largest ship, has its own particular name. Every respectable sailor must know these names! They are complicated and sometimes even funny. In fact, there are so many that there are special dictionaries just for marine words.

2. Icebreaker *Henry Larsen*, Canada (1988)
3. Fishing boat, Northern Europe
4. Luxury day cruiser 'Canados Gladiator 428', Italy
5. Vessel owned by the Dutch East India Company, The Netherlands (17th century)

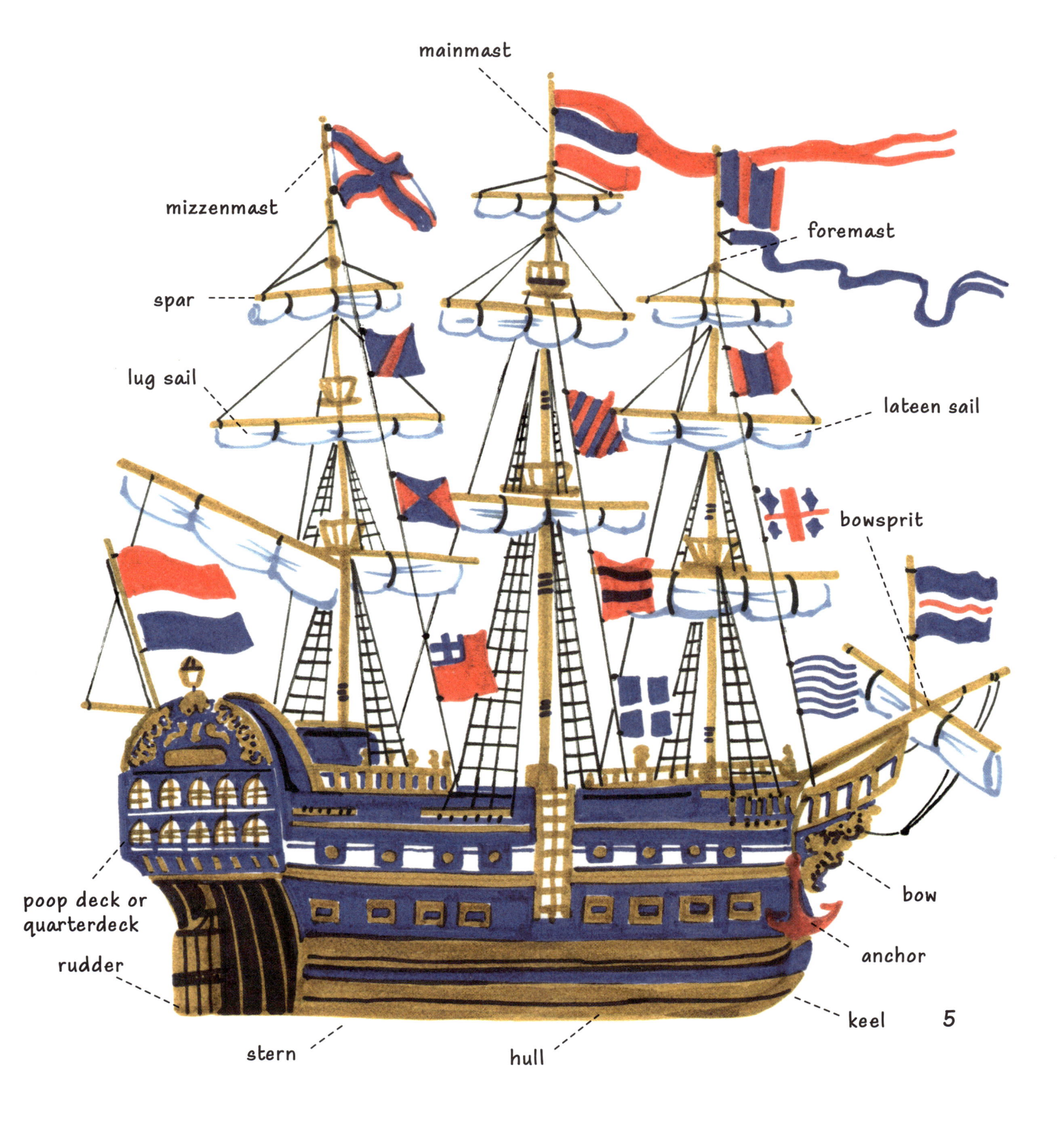

- mainmast
- mizzenmast
- spar
- lug sail
- foremast
- lateen sail
- bowsprit
- bow
- anchor
- keel
- hull
- stern
- rudder
- poop deck or quarterdeck

5

There are some big ships, really big ones, in fact absolutely enormous ones. The ship *Syracusia*, designed by Archimedes, was 110 metres long and could carry 500 people on board. It had a library and a temple dedicated to Aphrodite.

The Japanese 'atakebune' warships were so big that they could only move thanks to the efforts of hundreds of oarsmen, rowing with oars.

The cruise ships of today are a little like floating cities and can carry as many as 6,000 people on board.

6. *Syracusia*, Ancient Greek Sicily (240 BC)
7. Atakebune, Japan (16th century)
8. Oasis-class *Allure of the Seas*, Bahamas (2009)
9. *Mærsk Mc-Kinney Møller*, Denmark (2013)

8

Cargo ships exist that can load thousands of tons of goods, like the *Mærsk Mc-Kinney Møller*. This is one of the largest ships in the world at 400 metres long.

9

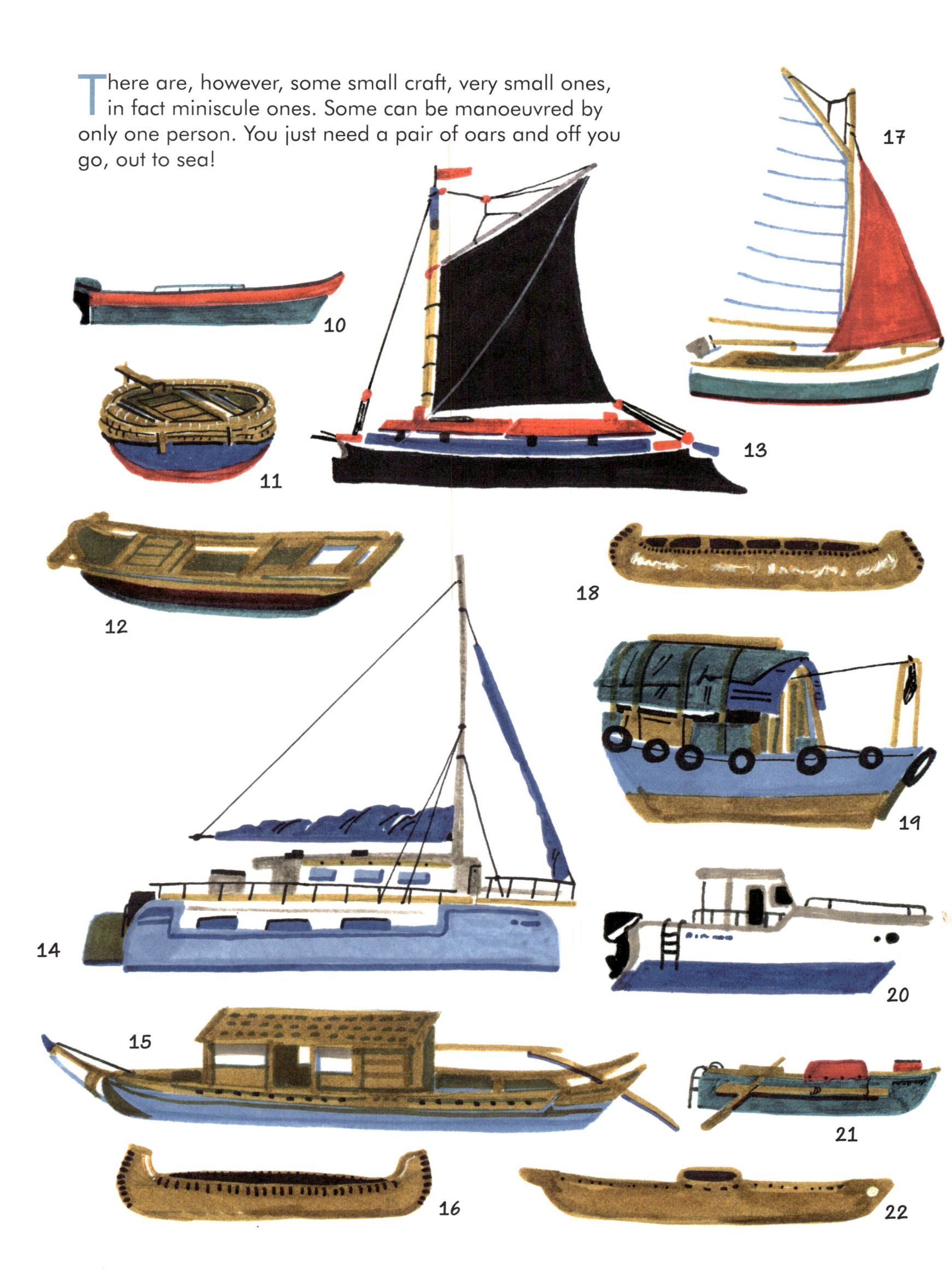

There are, however, some small craft, very small ones, in fact miniscule ones. Some can be manoeuvred by only one person. You just need a pair of oars and off you go, out to sea!

10
11
12
13
14
15
16
17
18
19
20
21
22

10. Ligurian gozzo, Italy
11. Coracle, South-East Asia/Wales
12. Fishing boat, Cat Ba Island, Vietnam
13. Wherry *Albion*, England (1898)
14. Catamaran, Europe
15. Sampan, Japan (1886)
16. Algonquin canoe, Canada, (18th century)
17. Gunter rig, UK
18. Nootka canoe, Canada (18th century)
19. Sampan, Hong Kong
20. Motorboat, Europe
21. Dinghy, Europe
22. Native kayak, Alaska, USA
23. Gondola, Venice, Italy
24. Haida dugout, Haida Gwaii, Canada (17th century)
25. Battana, Romagna, Italy
26. Raft, New Zealand
27. Pattino/Moscone (rowing catamaran), Italy
28. Quffa/Kuphar (coracle), Iraq
29. Jukung, Bali
30. Flybridge Yacht, Europe
31. Fishing boat, Senegal/Togo
32. Dhow, Zanzibar

There are ships that have been built to go underwater. If they are designed to travel in the deep, they are called 'submarines'. Smaller craft that go underwater for a short time but mainly stay on the surface attached to a platform or ship, are called 'submersibles'. Many craft of this type have been built for military and scientific purposes. Others have been imagined by writers, artists and singers. The American engineer, Robert Fulton, called his first tiny submarine, *Nautilus*. That same name was used many years later by the French author Jules Verne in his book *20,000 Leagues Under the Sea*, which told the story of a submarine as powerful as a spaceship. Who would have thought we would find so much traffic down at these depths?

33

34

35

36

33. *Yellow Submarine*, song by the Beatles, illustration by Heinz Edelmann, (1969)
34. Anorep I, a Jacques Cousteau submarine, Monaco (1966)
35. Triton 3300/3, submersible used by filmmakers, USA (2012)
36. 092 Xia–class nuclear submarine, China (1981)
37. SP-350 Denise, a Jacques Cousteau submarine, the 'Diving saucer' France (1959)
38. U-BOOT 96, submarine used in World War II, Germany (1935)
39. *Nautilus*, from Jules Verne's book *20,000 Leagues under the Sea* (1870)

There are some ships that can reach everywhere, really everywhere! Icebreakers are built especially to navigate on seas or on lakes whose surface is covered with ice. With their reinforced steel bows, they can break up the ice in front of them to move through and reach places that no other ship could ever even dream of reaching.

40. 'Arktika'–class, nuclear–powered icebreaker *Yamal*, Soviet Union, now Russia, (1989)

Many ships are used to transport goods from one part of the world to another and these are called 'cargo ships'. Today, ninety percent of ships on the oceans are in fact cargo ships. These ships have different shapes, sizes and 'holds', which is where the goods are stored, according to the type of cargo that they carry.

41

42

43

44

45

46

Ships that carry passengers, instead of cargo, also come in different shapes and sizes. Their size depends on the seas they cross and the number of people they carry.

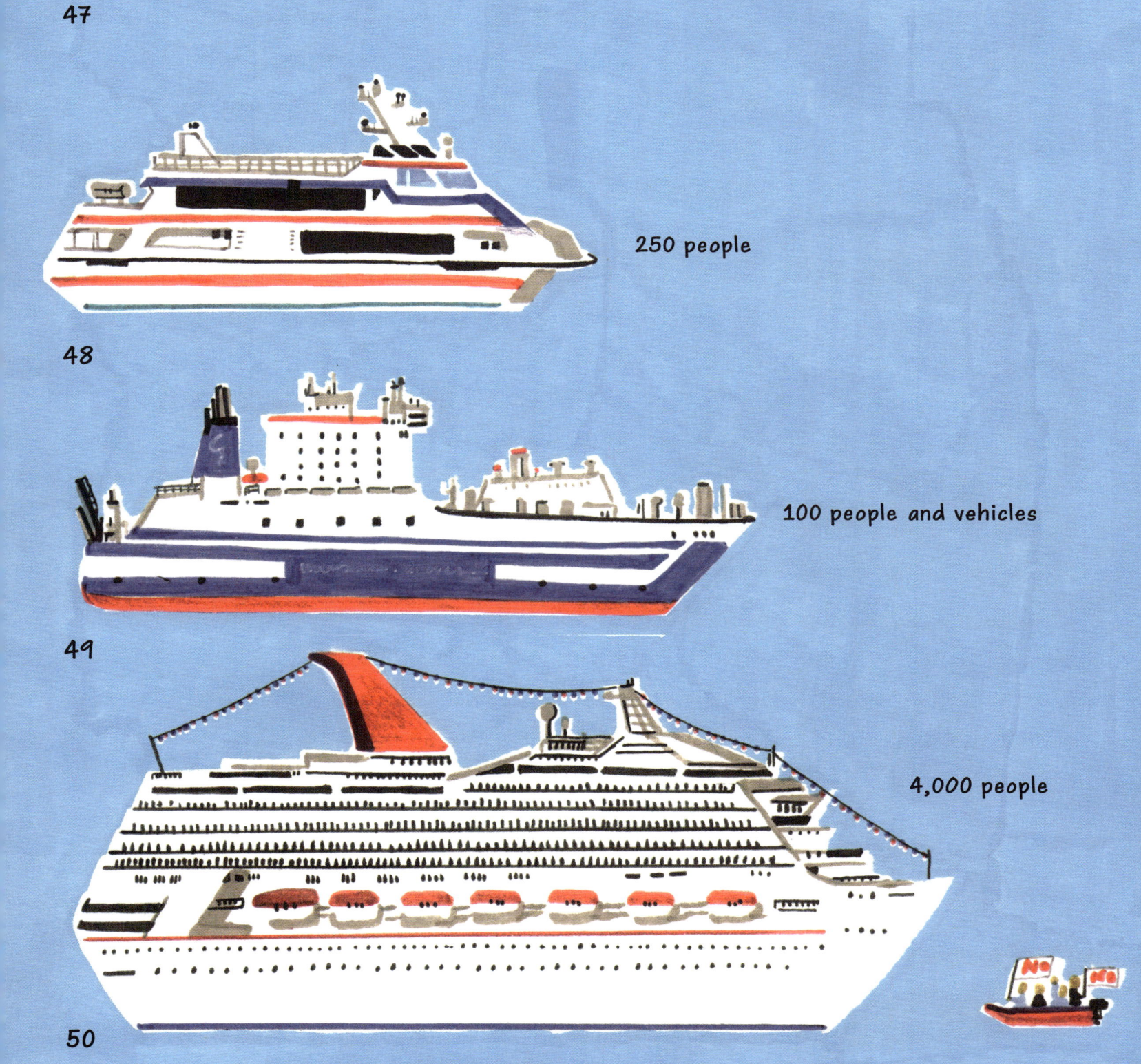

41. Roll-on, roll-off (RORO) ferry, UK
42. Tanker, China
43. Oil tanker, United Emirates
44. Container ship, Italy
45. Barge, Italy
46. Bulk carrier, USA
47. Vaporetto, a small ferry, Italy
48. Motor vessel (MV), Portugal
49. Car ferry, Italy
50. Cruise ship *Carnival Victory*, now *Carnival Radiance*, Panama (2000)

47 — 50 people

48 — 250 people

49 — 100 people and vehicles

50 — 4,000 people

Lastly, there are boats used for fishing that are called 'fishing smacks' or 'trawlers'. Depending on what they fish, fishermen and women use different craft. But as the characters in the book *Moby Dick* discover, not all creatures want to be caught!

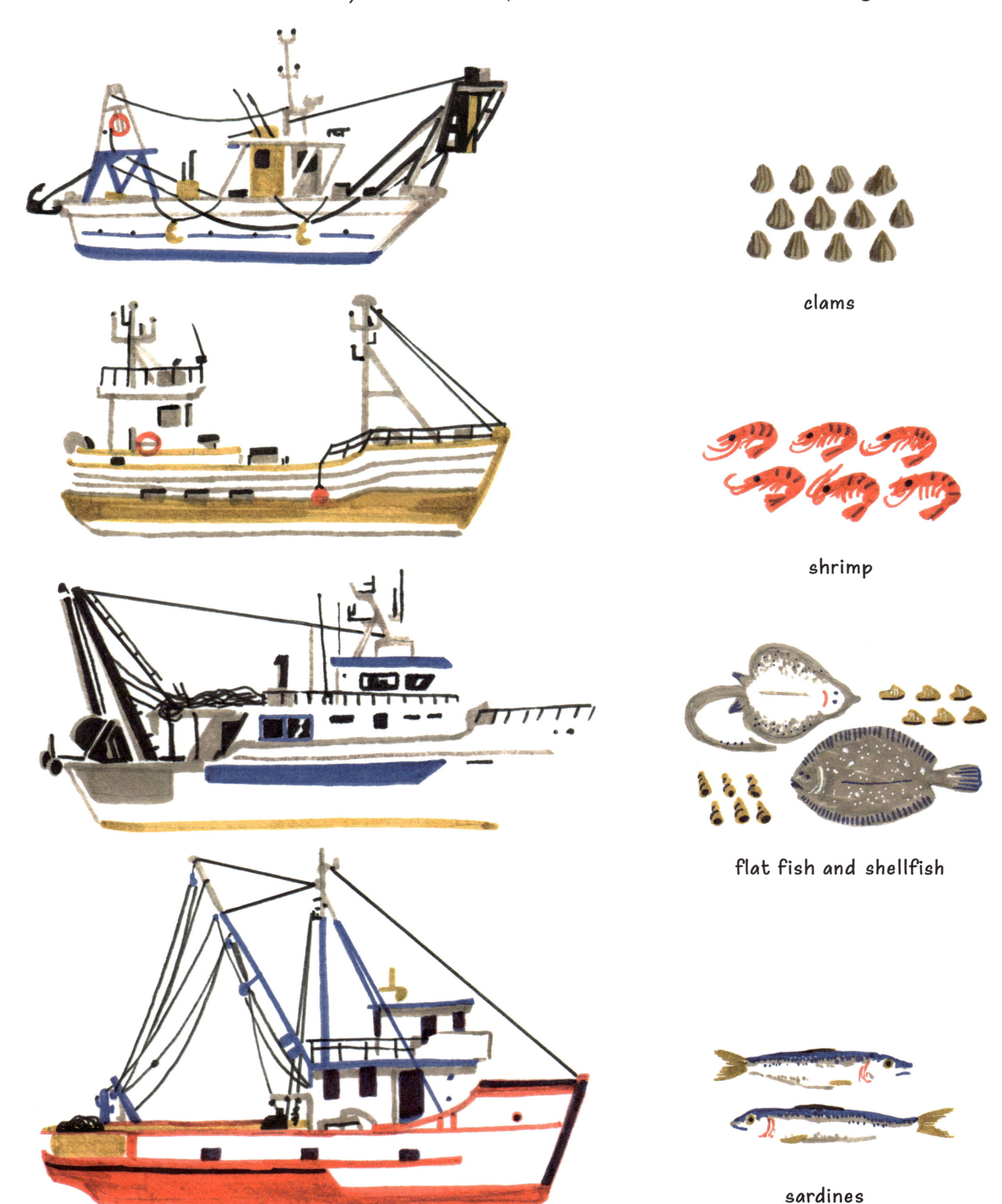

clams

shrimp

flat fish and shellfish

sardines

51. Whaler *Pequod*, Hermann Melville, *Moby Dick* (1851)

mackerel

tuna

red mullet

51

There are ships that were very famous in history even if they don't exist any more. The most famous of all is the British transatlantic liner, the *RMS Titanic*. During her maiden (first) voyage sailing to New York, on the night of 14th April 1912, she crashed into an iceberg. This collision sunk the ship and became one of the most disastrous shipwrecks in history. On board the *Titanic* there were 1,317 passengers and 913 members of the crew but only around 700 people were saved. This is such a famous story that there have been several films made about it! And the wreck of the *Titanic* is still on the seabed, around 3,800 metres down below.

52. Transatlantic passenger liner
RMS Titanic,
Belfast, Northern Ireland (1914)

There are other ships that are not as famous as the *Titanic* but are just as noteworthy. The 'sekibune' was a type of ship used by the powerful Japanese shōgun (military rulers) to travel really safely. It certainly looks very secure!

The 'geobukseon' of ancient Korea was a warship whose shape was just like that of an enormous, threatening turtle.

In Russia, there are even floating churches still in use today.

53. Sekibune, Japan (1467)
54. Geobukseon 'Turtle Ship', Korea (16th century)
55. Floating church, Russia
56. *Bucintoro* Venice, Italy (1722)

55

And the *Bucintoro* was the massive state barge of the Venetian Republic, used by the doges (rulers) during the most solemn ceremonies.

56

Ships have been built and used as a means of transport since the dawn of time by civilizations like the Egyptians, the Phoenicians, the Arabs, the Greeks and the Romans. In every corner of the world, ships have been used to transport men and enslaved peoples also, trade goods and fight battles. According to the Egyptians even the Sun used a special solar ship to cross the sky twice a day. Some of these ships have been navigating for hundreds of years and others are still used today.

Greek king Ulysses

57

58

59

60

61

62

63

64

57. Ulysses' ship, Homer, *The Odyssey*, (8th century BC)
58. Lorcha, Macao (17th century)
59. Liburna, Rome (100 – 001 BC)
60. Perahu Mayang, Java, (19th century)
61. Dromon, Byzantium (7th century)
62. Inuit umiak, Alaska, USA
63. Viking knarr, Norway (11th century)
64. Trireme, Greece/Rome, (200 – 101 BC)
65. Pentecontor, Phoenicia/Greece, (400 – 301 BC)
66. Bedar, Malaysia
67. Pirlapore Patli, Pakistan (15th century)
68. Galley, Venice, Italy (17th century)
69. Dhow, Arabian Peninsula
70. Mtepi, Zanzibar, (10th century)
71. Jalbut, Persian Gulf (12th century)
72. Solar ship, Egypt (1200 – 1101 BC)

Falcon god Horus

In ancient times ships travelled in search of new lands thanks not just to the hard work of oarsmen, but by harnessing the power of the wind. The first ships were equipped with just one mast and one sail. Then, in order to move bigger and bigger ships at a faster and faster speed, the number of sails increased to two, three, four, five and so on, until they added a great many of all shapes and sizes.

73

74

75

76

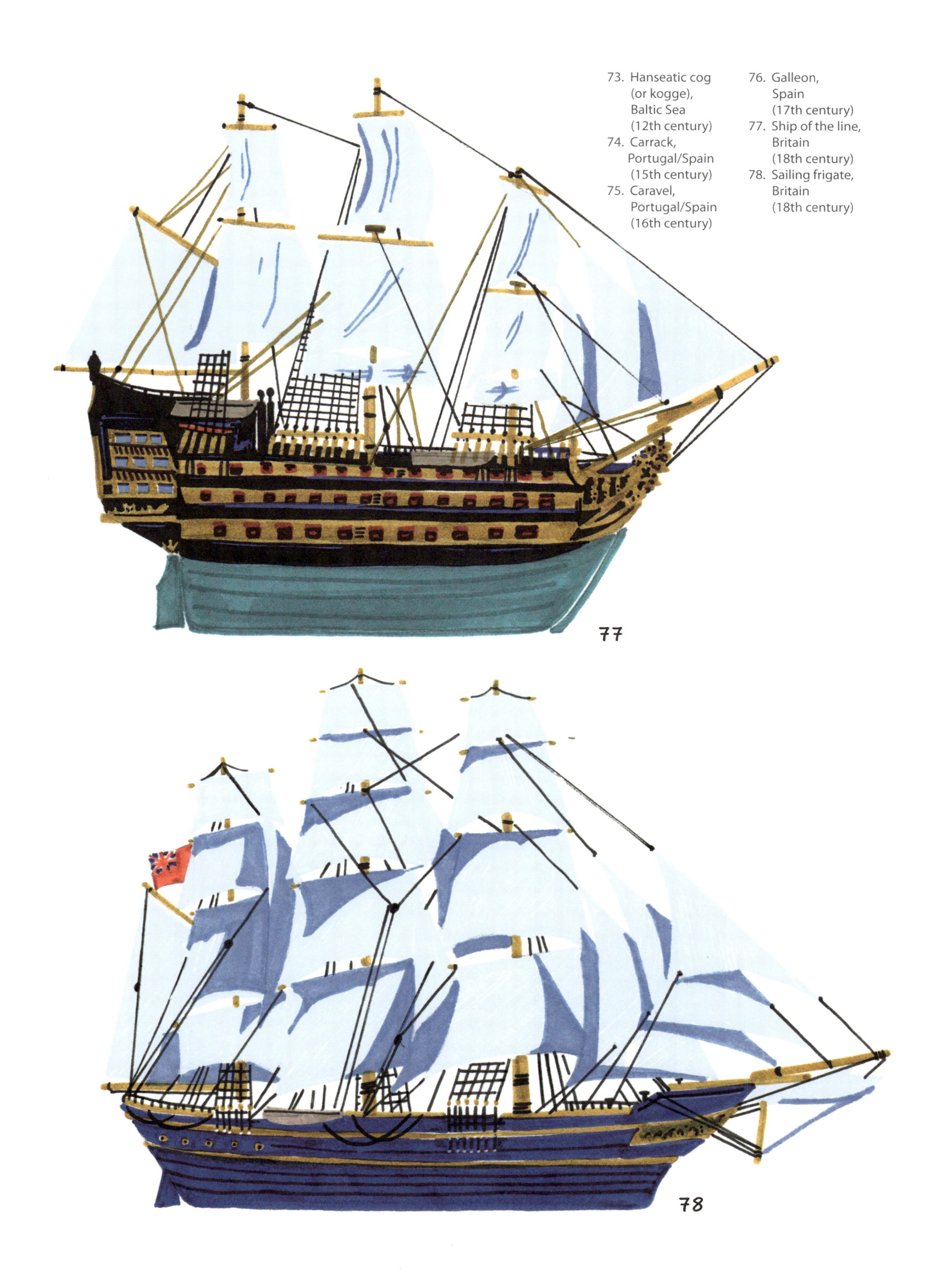

73. Hanseatic cog (or kogge), Baltic Sea (12th century)
74. Carrack, Portugal/Spain (15th century)
75. Caravel, Portugal/Spain (16th century)
76. Galleon, Spain (17th century)
77. Ship of the line, Britain (18th century)
78. Sailing frigate, Britain (18th century)

77

78

When there was no more space for new sails, James Watt and Robert Fulton invented the engine! The first steam ship, the *Clermont*, was in fact launched by Fulton in 1807, along the river Hudson, in the USA.

Although the *Clermont*, and its engine, represented a revolution in technology, it was almost immediately destroyed by the river boatmen who were afraid of losing their jobs to this dangerous competitor.

79. *Clermont*, New York, USA (1807)
80. *Mayflower*, USA (1849)
81. Giant steamboat, New Orleans, USA (1853)
82. *Monarch of the Mississippi*, USA (1870)

81

82

Throughout the centuries, ships were also used to fight fearsome battles and all sorts of wars. Some conflicts at sea involved hundreds of ships and thousands of men. Like, for example, the famous battle that took place on 7th October 1571 in the waters of Lepanto, Greece, between the Ottoman Empire and the Christian Holy League.

Or like the Battle of Trafalgar, fought between the fleet of the French Emperor, Napoleon Bonaparte, and the English Royal Navy, commanded by Admiral Horatio Nelson. Twenty-seven English warships defeated thirty-three Franco-Spanish warships without a single English ship being lost.

83. *HMS Royal Sovereign of the seas*, England (1805)

84. Warship *Indomptable*, France (1805)

For as long as goods and treasures have been transported by boat, pirates have been around trying to capture this loot for themselves. These pirates learned how to sail faster than other ships, and spent most of their time living at sea so that they could be ready for action. Famous people who were thought of as pirates by their enemies included Sir Francis Drake, who worked for Queen Elizabeth I of England, and Captain Henry Morgan, who raided Spanish ships in the Caribbean.

85

Sir Henry Morgan

86

87

88

Or Ching Shih, the most famous woman pirate in the world, also called the 'queen of the Chinese seas'.
In 1800, she controlled a fleet of 300 junks and more than 30,000 pirates.

Piracy still exists today in some parts of the world where pirates with fast speedboats attack ships and crews.

85. Galleon, Caribbean Sea, (17th century)
86. Xebec or Zebec, Mediterranean, (18th century)
87. Garay of the Banguingui people, Philippines (1890)
88. Wokou (pirate) ship, Korea
89. Junk, China (19th century)
90. Viking drakkar 'dragon' longship, Baltic Sea (14th century)
91. Lanong (pirate) ship of the Iranun people, Philippines (19th century)
92. RIB (rigid inflatable boat), Malacca Straits (20th century)
93. Speedboats, Somalia (20th century)

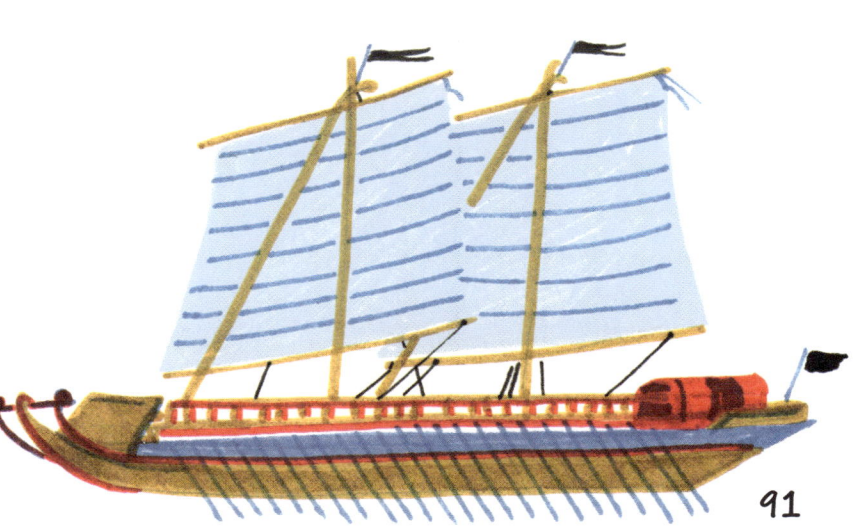

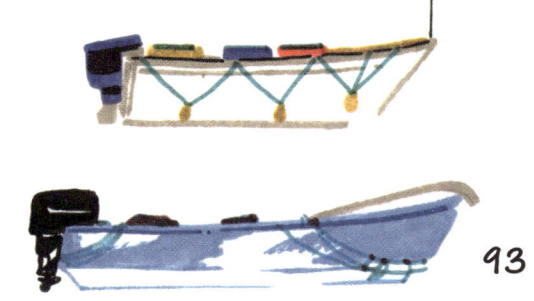

89

Ching Shih

90

91

92

93

There are also other types of pirate, like the musical pirates of Radio Caroline, for example. In 1964, big record companies controlled what music was played on the radio. So Mr Ronan O'Rahilly had the idea of starting a new radio station that played pop music all day, every day, from outside English territorial waters so they would not be blocked or fined by the authorities!

Today, there are still ships that are considered to be breaking the law. But some of these are trying to safeguard the marine habitats of fish, or offer help to people fleeing from wars or countries in difficulty.

94. *Radio Caroline*, England (1964)
95. *Sea-Watch 3*, Sea Watch, Germany (2018)
96. *Open Arms*, Open Arms, Spain
97. *Rainbow Warrior III* Greenpeace, Germany (2011)
98. *Steve Irwin*, Sea Shepherd, International (2007)
99. *Alan Kurdi*, Sea-Eye, Germany (2019)
100. *Mare Jonio*, Mediterranean, Saving Humans, Italy (2018)

From antiquity to the present day, there have always been those who have sailed the oceans to discover new lands and new types of living creatures. Like Charles Darwin, who set off on the brigantine *HMS Beagle*, captained by Robert FitzRoy, for a long voyage around the world. During his circumnavigation of the globe, Darwin catalogued hundreds of species. He observed their characteristics and differences and drew together this information to work out his famous theory of evolution.

a. Galapagos Giant Tortoise (Chelonoidis niger)   b. Galapagos Land Iguana (Conolophus subcristatus)   c. Blue-footed Booby (Sula nebouxii excisa)   d. Sally Lightfoot Crab (Percnon gibbesi)   e. Darwin's Finch (Geospizinae)   f. Galapagos Sea Lion (Zalophus wollebaeki)

101. Brigantine *HMS Beagle*, England (1820)

Between the end of the 19th century and the beginning of the 20th century, many people from Europe decided to set off on steamships and ocean liners to reach the Americas, seeking a better future. Among them were millions of Italians, Germans and Russians, including Jews escaping pogroms (attacks). Still today in various parts of the world, sometimes on rickety, unsafe vessels, there are people pushed by war or famine to take similar journeys across the sea in search of a safe place to live.

102. *RMS Queen Mary*, Southampton (1936)
103. *RMS Queen Elizabeth*, Southampton (1938)
104. *SS Cristofero Colombo*, Italy (1953)
105. *SS Andrea Doria*, Italy (1953)

Home means different things to different people – to some people home means a boat that is shaped like a house, or even a house that is shaped like a boat! In some parts of the world, like Kashmir or Hong Kong, there are even whole floating villages. A houseboat is a boat that is designed for living in all the time. Sometimes these houseboats are anchored to the shore but sometimes they can also travel up and down rivers and across lakes, constantly looking for new places to moor for the night.

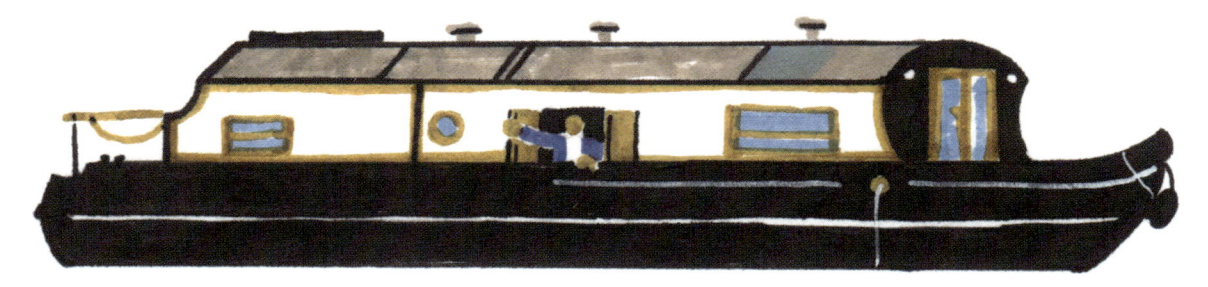

London, England

Arnhem, The Netherlands

Aberdeen, Hong Kong

Kettuvallam, India

Srinagar, Kashmir

Spreehafen, Hamburg, Germany

Amazonia, Brazil

Amsterdam, The Netherlands

Illinois, USA

Uros, Peru

Now that you have learned all about the secrets and hidden histories of boats, there is nothing left for you to do but to set sail yourself. You may only manage an imaginary voyage in your own bathtub, and that is fine, or you might get the chance to glide gracefully across a calm lake in a city park, or maybe you will be lucky enough to bravely brace the wild waves on the open ocean – now that you have read this book, you will be more than ready for the adventure that awaits.